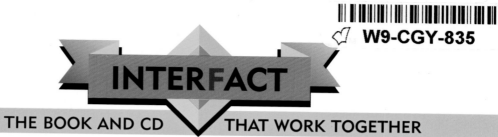

INTERFACT

THE BOOK AND CD THAT WORK TOGETHER

POLAR LANDS

TWO CAN™

LONDON ■ PRINCETON

www.two-canpublishing.com

**Published by Two-Can Publishing,
43–45 Dorset Street, London W1U 7NA**

© Two-Can Publishing 2001, 1998

For information on Two-Can books and multimedia,
call (0)20 7224 2440, fax (0)20 7224 7005, or visit our
Web site at http://www.two-canpublishing.com

Created by
act-two
346 Old Street
London EC1V 9RB

ISBN 1-85434-913-9

2 4 6 8 10 9 7 5 3 1

A catalogue record for this book is available from the British Library

Photograph credits: Robert Harding Picture Library: front cover; Ardea Ltd: p.7, p.12, p.15, p.16, p.17 (t),
p.19 (b); Bruce Coleman: p.6 p.18, p.23, p.25; NHPA: p.8, p.9, p.17 (b), p.26; Survival Anglia: p.11,
p.14 (t), p.19 (t), p.24; B&C Alexander: p.14 (b), p.20, p.27. All illustrations by Francis Mosley.

Every effort has been made to acknowledge correctly and contact the source of
each picture and Two-Can Publishing apologises for any unintentional errors
or omissions which will be corrected in future editions of this book.

Printed in Hong Kong by Wing King Tong

INTERFACT

THE BOOK AND CD ∨ THAT WORK TOGETHER

INTERFACT will have you hooked in minutes –
and that's a fact!

The disk is packed with interactive activities, puzzles, quizzes and games that are great fun to do and full of interesting facts.

Build an interactive food web and learn what different polar creatures eat.

Build the food web by dragging the icons into position with your mouse

Open the book and discover more fascinating information highlighted with lots of full-colour illustrations and photographs.

Read about the fascinating creatures that live in the polar oceans.

To get the most out of **INTERFACT**, use the book and disk together. Look out for the special signs, called Disk Links and Bookmarks. To find out more, turn to page 43.

23

BOOKMARK

DISK LINK
Delve deeper into the history of the poles and take a trip in the TIME MACHINE.

Once you've clicked on to **INTERFACT**, you'll never look back.

LOAD UP!
Go to **page 40** to find out how to load your disk and click into action.

What's on the disk

HELP SCREEN

Learn how to use the disk in no time at all.

Get to grips with the controls and find out how to use:

- arrow keys
- reading boxes
- 'hot' words

FOOD FOR THOUGHT

Create your own polar food webs on screen!

Build an interactive food web for the Arctic or the Antarctic. Use your mouse to drag the animals and plants around the screen and see if you can work out who eats what.

CHILL OUT

It's time to put your knowledge of polar lingo to the test.

This little penguin is stranded on a melting iceberg and it's up to you to rescue him. Work out a mystery polar word before time runs out and stop him falling into the icy waters.

SNOWBALL FIGHT

The polar lands quiz. It's a battle of brains – and snowballs!

Find out how much you know with this quiz on the polar lands. Each correct answer earns you snowballs to throw at your opponent. Play against a friend or challenge the computer!

POLES APART

What's the difference between the Arctic and the Antarctic?

Try to match up each of the interactive icons on the screen with the correct polar landscape. Discover the important differences between the two polar lands.

EXPLORE THE POLAR LANDS

Take a look at an interactive polar landscape.

Use your mouse to take a close-up look at the Arctic and the Antarctic. Discover all you need to know about the animals and plants that survive in this incredible environment.

ALL THE ANSWERS

Introducing Sidney the Seal and Alberta the Albatross.

Sidney the Seal is full of questions about the polar lands – just like you! Pick a question you want Sid to ask then click on Alberta the Albatross to find out the answer.

TIME MACHINE

Get the lowdown on the history of the polar lands.

In 1959, 12 countries signed the Antarctic Treaty. According to the treaty, Antarctica may only be used for peaceful purposes and scientists must share all their discoveries.

Go on a journey of discovery and travel back in time. Learn about the fascinating past of the polar lands from prehistoric times right up to the present day.

What's in the book

Looking at the poles

Few places in the world are as harsh and desolate as the areas surrounding the North and South Poles. And few places are as beautiful. For much of the year, both areas are freezing cold, with fierce winds blowing and thick snow and ice on the ground. As it grows colder, even the seas freeze.

It is hard to imagine that anything could survive in such an extreme climate. However, many plants, animals and people have made this frozen habitat their home.

In the summer months – May to July at the North Pole and November to January at the South Pole – the Sun shines, even at midnight. But in winter, the poles remain almost permanently dark.

In the short Arctic summers, the snow and ice recede, leaving pools of **meltwater** on the ground. The land bursts into life. Flowers and plants grow and the air is filled with insects. Creatures mate and find safe places to raise their young.

▶ Plants in the polar lands spend most of the year under snow. Their seeds are hardy and do not **germinate** until the short summer when conditions are exactly right for growth.

DISK LINK
What's the difference between the Arctic and the Antarctic? Find out in POLES APART!

▼ A large **iceberg** floats in the sea during the Antarctic summer. It is evening but at this time of year, the sky is never very dark.

Where in the world?

The poles are at the top and bottom of the Earth. The Sun's rays have to travel further to reach the poles. As a result, they receive less of the Sun's warmth than anywhere else. This is why the polar lands are the coldest places in the world.

The North Pole lies in the middle of a frozen sea called the Arctic Ocean. It is surrounded by Northern Europe, Russia and North America. The most northerly point where trees will grow is about 2,300km from the North Pole. Between the **tree line** and the **icecap**, are regions of rough terrain called **tundra**. The ground is always frozen beneath the tundra, even in the summer. This layer of frozen earth is called **permafrost**.

The huge continent of Antarctica lies around the South Pole. It is permanently covered in a thick shield of ice. Snow and ice lie deeper here than anywhere else in the world.

HISTORY OF THE POLES

● **150–170 million years ago**
The poles are not frozen. The South Pole probably lies over low ground and the North Pole over the sea.

● **60–70 million years ago**
Shifts in the Earth's **plates** cause the polar lands to move to the positions where they are now. They begin to cool.

● **5–6 million years ago**
Changes in the climate and in the heat received from the Sun bring new conditions of snow and ice.

NORTH POLE FACTS

● The Arctic Ocean is surrounded by land. Consequently, currents from warmer seas cannot reach it and raise the temperature.

● The Ancient Greeks named the Arctic after a group of stars known as 'Arktos', meaning the Great Bear.

● In 1909, Robert Peary and Matthew Henson became the first European people to reach the North Pole.

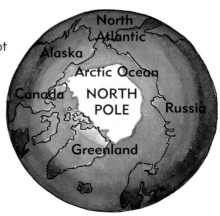

The polar lands were not always so cold. Fossils of trees, plants and animals in Antarctica show that it once had a much warmer climate. Over millions of years, the Earth's land masses have moved and the temperature has changed. This has brought about the freezing conditions at the poles today.

▲ A herd of caribou makes its annual journey to the rich feeding grounds of the Arctic tundra.

DISK LINK
Delve deeper into the history of the poles and take a trip in the TIME MACHINE.

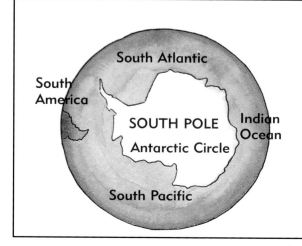

SOUTH POLE FACTS

● 75 per cent of the world's fresh water is stored in **glaciers** and most of this lies in the Antarctic icecap.

● The Antarctic can be called a desert because it receives less than 25cm of rain or snow per year.

● In 1911, the Norwegian explorer, Roald Amundsen, beat Britain's Robert Scott to the South Pole by one month.

Frozen features

A quarter of the world's oceans and seas are affected by ice every year. Around the poles, the sea actually freezes. **Icebergs** from polar regions also float across other oceans. One iceberg from Antarctica almost reached Rio de Janeiro in Brazil – a journey of 5,500km.

Ice covers most of the land around the South Pole. This blanket of ice forms **glaciers** that spread across the continent until they reach the sea. Sometimes, the long, icy fingers of a glacier break and vast chunks of ice fall into the ocean. This is how icebergs are formed.

◄ The Paradise Bay Glacier is in Antarctica. Sections break off from its craggy cliffs and plummet into the clear waters below to form icebergs.

In 1912, an ocean liner called *Titanic* collided with an iceberg off the coast of Canada. The ship sank with the loss of 1,522 lives. Ever since the disaster, the International Ice Patrol has monitored icebergs and alerted ships to danger.

Icebergs are made from frozen fresh water but the salty ocean around the poles also freezes. This reaches a peak during the months of February and March when there is about 12 million km^2 of sea-ice in the Arctic Ocean and three million km^2 off Antarctica.

As the sea freezes, a greasy film appears to cover the surface of the water. Wisps of smoky vapour rise from the surface and, as the sea water turns to ice, salt is pushed above the surface in beautiful crystals called **ice flowers**.

DIFFERENT SORTS OF ICE

● Pieces of frozen sea water are called **floes**. When lots of floes gather together, they form **pack ice**. Pack ice is pushed around the polar seas by the wind and ocean currents.

● The ice at the outer edges of a glacier is usually very dense and very old. The ice in some glaciers was formed many thousands of years ago.

● **Tabular** icebergs have flat tops. Some are several kilometres long and are sometimes used by scientists as convenient research bases.

● Large pieces of ice break off from icebergs to form floating chunks known as **bergy bits**. Smaller fragments of floating ice are called **growlers**.

Animal life

Despite the bleakness of the polar lands, many animals live here. Some remain all year round while others are only summer visitors.

The only permanent residents on the Antarctic mainland are insects. Penguins and seals make their homes on the ice at the edge of the ocean and the waters of Antarctica are teeming with life.

An enormous variety of animals live in the Arctic, from tiny shrews to huge polar bears. Native species are well adapted to make good use of the short summer and to protect themselves against the long, cold winter.

Many polar animals are larger than similar creatures in warmer climates. They have short legs, long hair and an undercoat of dense fur. Their tails are short and the pads on their feet are furry.

▲ The stoat grows a white **pelt** during the winter for **camouflage**. This helps it to hunt and avoid predators.

▼ Polar bear cubs are born in pairs and stay with their mother for up to two years. They live as long as 33 years in the wild.

▶ Seals come in many shapes and sizes. They are superbly adapted to life in the water. Seals are sleek, torpedo-shaped animals with flippers in place of legs. These help them move easily through the water. Their bodies are covered in a thick layer of **blubber** that protects their internal organs from the cold. This blubber also provides the seals with energy. Seals can live off their reserves of blubber when there is no food available.

Life in the Arctic is a delicate balancing act. The number of plants affects the number of small animals which affects the number of **carnivores**. The carnivores eat the small animals – which, in turn, affects the number of plants!

DISK LINK
Some words on this page will help you to save the penguin when you play **CHILL OUT!**

◀ A pack of wolves follows its leader into the **tree line**. A pack is a family group consisting of about eight members. Most wolves have grey fur but the fur of Arctic wolves is usually white. Their coats are long and thick to help keep them warm. A wolf can see and smell its prey over 1.6km away. Wolves can eat up to 9kg of food at one time but they can also go without eating for two weeks or longer.

Birdland

Winter in the polar lands is too cold for most birds but many species arrive during the summer. The Arctic tern has the longest journey of any polar visitor. It flies from summer at one pole to summer at the other and covers a distance of about 30,000km every year. Other birds include ducks such as widgeon, eider and teal, as well as geese, larks and pipits. On the ground lie pools of melted ice and snow where millions of mosquitoes and other insects flourish. The humming air is a feast for birds!

Some birds spend winter on the **subarctic** wastes of the **tundra**. They survive by searching for roots and berries under the snow or by feeding on other birds, small mammals or insects. The ptarmigan, snowy owl, raven and Arctic redpoll live close to the **tree line** in this region.

Unlike many other birds, lots of penguins spend their entire lives in the Antarctic. They are protected from the cold by a thick layer of **blubber** and waterproof feathers. Some penguins can dive as deep as 260m underwater in search of fish.

King penguins spend up to a month at sea searching for food to feed their chicks. Back on shore, the penguins cluster together in groups. The cold penguins from the edge of the group swap places with the warmer birds in the centre every few minutes. Young king penguins soon grow into enormous fluffy chicks. Some chicks weigh up to 12kg!

DISK LINK
How many different kinds of penguin live in Antarctica? Find out when you EXPLORE THE POLAR LANDS.

◀ The largest member of the penguin family is the emperor. It stands over 1m tall and weighs up to 40kg. The male **incubates** the eggs in a pouch on his feet. He will go as long as two months without eating while looking after his chick.

▲ A black-browed albatross flies over the southern ocean. It has long, thin wings that help it to glide through the air.

▼ Puffins fly to the Arctic Circle during the summer and nest among the rocky cliffs surrounding the frozen ocean.

Sea life

Icebergs are not the only things you will find in the polar oceans. The water is cold but it is teeming with life. As well as the creatures that live in the sea, many other animals take to the water in search of food. These include polar bears, penguins and seals.

In the Antarctic, currents from warmer seas encourage many varieties of colourful lifeforms. Bright orange sea spiders, delicate anemones, fronds of primitive weeds, worms and other strange plants and creatures are found on the sea floor.

Strange, ghostly fish live here too, such as the pale ice fish or the transparent deep-sea angler. These fish live in deep water. Very little light filters through to the depths so these creatures have no need for bright colouring.

AN ARCTIC FEAST

Sperm whales are **toothed whales**. They eat fish and squid.

Seals also feed on fish and squid.

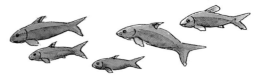

Some types of fish are **herbivores**. Others are carnivores and eat krill and other fish.

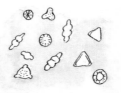 

Plankton are microscopic organisms. Some plankton are tiny plants, others are microscopic animals.

Krill are small sea creatures that feed on plankton.

◀ Krill are tiny crustaceans, similar to shrimps. Some countries have begun fishing krill to use as human food. This threatens the creatures of the polar lands that rely on krill as a food source.

Some of these bizarre creatures have special organs in their bodies that produce light. This enables them to see in the dark depths near the sea bed.

The largest marine animals, whales, are also found in the waters around the polar lands. Biggest of all are the blue whales which grow up to 30m long and weigh up to 150,000kg. There are two groups of whales – toothed whales, which feed on fish and squid, and **baleen whales** which feed on krill. Baleen whales have a series of bony plates in their mouths that helps them to filter out the krill from the water.

DISK LINK
Build the interactive food webs to learn what's on the menu in the polar regions in
FOOD FOR THOUGHT.

▲ A killer whale **breaching**. Killer whales are, in fact, members of the dolphin family. They can swim at 40km/h. They live in all oceans but prefer the colder waters around the polar lands.

◀ This giant sea spider has 10 legs and lives on the ocean floor near Antarctica. The bodies of most sea spiders are so small that some of their food has to be digested in their legs!

People of the poles

Antarctica has no native human inhabitants. The only people here are scientists who brave the region to carry out experiments.

People have lived in the Arctic for thousands of years. Some still live as **nomads**, following the herds of animals that provide their livelihood. Today, however, a great number of the native peoples have made their homes in one of the modern settlements.

The Inuit people have adapted to life in the Poles and are the most widespread group of Arctic inhabitants.

▼ Igloos are still built by Inuit people for use as overnight resting places on long hunting trips. They are made from slabs of ice, cut to size and placed together. Light is produced by burning whale or seal oil in a small container. This also helps to keep the igloo warm inside.

DISK LINK
Want to ask a question about polar people? Click on Sidney the Seal in ALL THE ANSWERS!

They live in North America and the Russian Federation. Some Inuit people still drive sledges pulled by dogs and wear clothes made from animal skins. Most prefer to ride over the **icecap** on engine-driven snowmobiles and to wear modern anoraks even though the stitched skins are, in fact, warmer.

Recent changes in the way that Eastern Europe is governed mean that Arctic people are now able to travel more freely than under the old laws. Today, the closely-related Inuit tribes of Alaska and Russia are allowed to meet without regard to political boundaries.

Hopefully, the peoples of the North will find it easier to fish and hunt where the animals wander and not where governments want them to live.

PEOPLE FACTS

● Viking explorers were the first people from Europe to meet Inuit people.

● Arctic people eat mostly fish and meat as there is very little plant life.

● More than 100,000 Inuit live in four countries along the Arctic coast.

▲ This is an Inuit man wearing his boots, leggings, trousers, jacket and mittens. These are made from caribou, bear or wolf skins. The clothes are loose to trap a layer of warm air underneath. The seams are tightly sewn to make the garments waterproof.

Watching the weather

Polar lands are particularly useful places to study the weather. **Meteorologists** always monitor the poles with interest. Conditions in the Arctic and Antarctic affect the climate all over the world. For example, when cold air from the poles meets warm air from tropical regions, it can change the weather where you live.

▼ If the polar **icecaps** were to melt because of global warming, many countries around the world would be flooded. Important cities including those on the map below could be lost beneath the rising waters.

THE EARTH'S ATMOSPHERE

ionosphere

stratosphere

troposphere

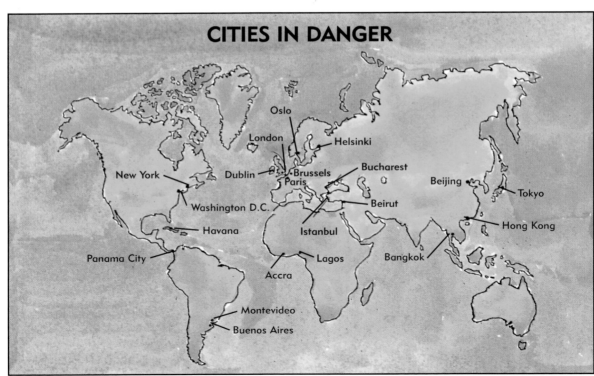

CITIES IN DANGER

Oslo
London
Helsinki
New York
Dublin
Brussels
Paris
Bucharest
Beijing
Tokyo
Washington D.C.
Beirut
Hong Kong
Havana
Istanbul
Panama City
Lagos
Bangkok
Accra
Montevideo
Buenos Aires

Scientists are also very concerned about the **ozone layer** above the poles. This is the layer in the Earth's stratosphere that protects us from the Sun's harmful ultraviolet rays. It is being destroyed by man-made chemicals such as chlorofluorocarbons (known as CFCs for short) that are used in some aerosol sprays, foam packaging and fridges. The problem is worse above the poles where holes have appeared in the ozone layer.

Scientists at the poles investigate long-term changes in the Earth's climate, such as global warming. By examining ice that formed hundreds or even thousands of years ago, they can discover what the temperature of the Earth was like and if it is changing.

▲ The aurora borealis, caused by the entry of solar particles into the Earth's magnetic field, is a beautiful sight seen mainly near the North Pole. A similar display in the Antarctic is known as the aurora australis.

HOW YOU CAN HELP SAVE THE EARTH

● Stop using aerosols that contain CFCs. These chemical destroy the ozone layer. Look out for alternatives which are now widespread in supermarkets. Most are labelled 'ozone friendly' or 'CFC-free'.

● An average car powered by petrol produces its own weight in carbon dioxide fumes every year. Carbon dioxide is one of the major greenhouse gases responsible for global warming. So, why not try to walk or cycle more rather than travelling in a car?

Global warming is a potential ecological disaster. It is caused by **greenhouse gases** building up in the Earth's atmosphere. These gases act as a blanket and trap more of the Sun's heat around the Earth. As a result, the temperature of the Earth could rise.

At present, polar temperatures rise only to 10°C at the very height of the summer period. If the temperature in the polar lands were to rise by more than five per cent at the poles, the ice would melt and sea levels across the world could rise drastically. Low-lying cities, such as London and New York, as well as whole countries like the Netherlands and Bangladesh, could be flooded. At these temperatures, many of the animals and plants in the polar regions would die out too.

Exploiting the poles

The first outsiders to see the potential for money making at the poles arrived during the 19th century. They killed many whales for their meat and **blubber** which was used in a variety of products from soap to oil. Seals, particularly fur seals, were trapped for their attractive **pelts**. Penguins were killed because oil from their bodies was used in lamps.

Today, international agreements are in force that protect the creatures of the poles from hunters. A few animals are still killed each year for scientific purposes and native peoples are also permitted to hunt a small number of animals.

However, the animals now face other dangers. Polar bears, for example, are scavengers and sometimes become dependent on scientific bases for scraps of food. They are often seen in rubbish dumps, where they may eat unsuitable things or cut themselves. Some bears lose the will to hunt altogether.

But it is not just the animals that are in danger. Some scientists fear that dust and grime from the oil refineries and other industries in the Arctic might make the ice dirty and darker.

This could make global warming worse and might lead to a dangerous increase in the Earth's temperature.

DISK LINK
Read this page carefully! It will help you earn the ammunition you'll need in SNOWBALL FIGHT.

POLAR RESOURCES

● 98% of Antarctica is covered by thick ice but beneath may lie valuable deposits of rubies and other minerals.

● Reserves of oil and natural gas lie under Alaska, Arctic Canada and Siberia. Further oil deposits are found off the coast of Greenland, on the Arctic shores of the North Atlantic and in parts of the southern ocean.

● Oil spilled from a tanker accident in Alaska in 1989 caused the death of many birds and other animals.

◄ The white bones of dead whales remind us of the years when these creatures were hunted mercilessly. The bowhead was even called the 'right whale' because it was so easy to catch.

▲ A polar bear forages among the litter of a settlement in northern Canada. He may be poisoned or injured and he also poses a serious threat to local inhabitants.

The glaring white surface of the **icecap** at each pole reflects some of the Sun's energy back into space. This helps to stop the temperature of the Earth's atmosphere increasing.

Dark colours, on the other hand, soak up the Sun's warmth. This is why wearing dark clothes in summer makes you feel hot while light clothes keep you cool.

If large areas of the Arctic icecap get darker as a result of pollution, the effects on our environment could be disastrous!

Saving the poles

It is important that people realise the value of the polar lands. Polar animals and plants will die if the temperature in these regions rises by even a small amount. What is more, if the poles were to melt, the impact on the rest of the world would be devastating.

Measures have been taken to establish the polar regions as places of special scientific interest rather than as lands to be exploited. The Antarctic Treaty, concerning the ownership of the South Pole's lands, has now been agreed by most governments.

Even industry has taken steps to avoid further damage to these beautiful environments. Special ice roads have been built to stop plants being crushed under the wheels of heavy vehicles.

Similarly, oil and gas pipelines are built like bridges and raised above the ground. Despite the continuing encroachment on the lands of the poles, the caribou in the north may continue their migration in peace.

DISK LINK
EXPLORE THE POLAR LANDS and find out even more about our feathery friends, the penguins!

▲ This is a rookery of king penguins. These creatures have adapted well to the extreme cold of Antarctica but they may not survive if the poles become warmer as a result of global warming.

▶ These are the snow-crusted ridges of Greenland. The world would lose one of its great natural beauties if we allow the destruction of the polar **icecaps**.

Crow steals some daylight

For thousands of years, people have told stories about the world around them. Often, these stories try to explain something that people do not really understand, like how the world began, or where light comes from. This tale is told by the Inuit people who live in the polar lands of Northern Canada.

Long ago, in the northern lands where the Inuit live, there was no daylight. The people ate, slept, hunted and cooked, all in darkness. There was no light to tell the people when it was day and when it was night, so they all got up at different times. When they needed to see they would light little seal-oil lamps which gave off a small glimmer of light, but

day long. The people of this land could see without using lamps or fires and could spot animals in the distance. This helped them to stay out of danger and to hunt for food more easily. The villagers were amazed at what the crow said and began to realise how difficult their lives were without light.

"When we go fishing," said one,

scarcely enough to see by.

In one village lived a wise, old crow. He used to tell the Inuit people stories of the far-off lands that he had visited on his travels. One day, he told them about a distant land where there was light all

"we have to cut a hole in the ice and then shine a light into it to see if there are any fish there. The fish see the light and they are scared off. If it were light all the time, we would be able to see the fish before they saw us."

"And without light," said another, "we might walk straight into the arms of a polar bear before we even realise that it's there. If it were light all the time, we would be able to see them in the distance and keep away."

All the villagers begged the crow to go to the land of daylight and fetch them some light. At first the crow refused, because it was such a long journey. But the villagers had always been very good to him, so eventually he agreed.

It was a very long journey indeed and when, at last, the crow reached the lands where the sky was bright with daylight, he sank to the ground, exhausted. He found himself in a village not so very different from the one he had left. In the middle of the village was a house from which daylight shone brightly.

"Aha!" thought the crow. "That is where the daylight comes from."

As he watched, a woman walked up to the house. The crow flew over to the door, shook off his skin and turned himself into a speck of dust, which settled on the woman's dress as she went into the house.

Inside the house, a great chief sat watching a baby playing on a fur rug. As the woman passed, she bent down and tickled the baby. She didn't notice the tiny speck of dust fall from her dress and into the little baby's ear. It was the crow of course!

The baby tugged at its ear, which tickled dreadfully, and began to cry,

whereupon the chief and the woman leapt up and began to fuss over it.

"Ask for some daylight," whispered the speck of dust.

So the baby cried for some daylight. The chief picked up a carved wooden box, placed it before the baby and opened the lid. Inside were seven, glowing balls of daylight. The chief took out one and gave it to the baby. The baby was so delighted with its new toy that all its tears were gone at once.

"Ask for a string to be tied to the ball," whispered the speck of dust in the baby's ear.

And the baby began to cry for a string to be tied to the beautiful ball of daylight.

As soon as the chief had tied a string to the ball and given it to the baby, the little speck of dust whispered in the baby's ear again.

"Move over to the doorway."

The baby crawled over to the doorway of the hut, trailing the ball of daylight on its string and sat, framed by the arch, with daylight shining brightly all around.

Gradually the baby moved further and further out of the house, dangling the ball, right to the very spot where the crow had left his skin. Quick as a flash, the speck of dust fell out of the baby's ear, picked up the skin and became the crow again. The crow snatched the string from the baby and flew off, carrying away the bright ball. All the villagers came rushing out of their houses. They threw stones at the crow and tried to shoot him down

with their bows and arrows. But the crow flew off towards his home much too fast for them.

When, at last, the crow came to the land of the Inuit, he broke off a piece of daylight from the ball over each village that he passed and let it fall to the ground. Finally, after much travelling, he reached the village that he had set off from. Then he let go of the string he was holding and all that was left of the ball of daylight fell to the ground and shattered into lots of tiny fragments. Shafts of light streamed into all the houses. The villagers rushed out of their houses to thank the crow for his wonderful gift.

The crow told the story of how he had stolen the light. He explained to all the villagers that he had not brought enough light for them to have daylight all the time, but only enough for half the year and that the other half of the year they would have to spend in darkness.

"But if I had brought enough daylight for it to be always light," he said, "you would have had as much trouble as you did when it was always dark!"

True or false?

Which of these facts are true and which are false?
If you have read this book carefully, you will know the answers!

1. Summer falls between May and July at both poles.

2. No plants grow in the polar lands.

3. Plants and animals once lived in a warmer climate on Antarctica.

4. The Arctic was named by the ancient Greeks after the constellation of Orion the Hunter.

5. Roald Amundsen was the first man to reach the South Pole.

6. The Titanic sank in 1912, after running into a whale.

7. Large fragments from an ice sheet are called bergy growlers.

8. The largest, permanent residents on the Antarctic ice sheet are insects.

9. A male emperor penguin will go as long as two months without food.

10. Polar bear cubs are born two at a time.

11. Arctic people are mostly vegetarian.

12. A car running on petrol releases its own weight in carbon dioxide fumes every year.

ANSWERS: 1.F 2.F 3.T 4.F 5.T 6.F 7.F 8.T 9.T 10.T 11.F 12.T

Glossary

Baleen whales have curtains of bony plates in their mouths. These allow them to filter krill out of the water.

Bergy bits are large, floating chunks of ice that are roughly the same size as an average house.

Blubber is the name for the thick layer of fat on animals such as seals, walruses, penguins and whales. This layer helps to protect them against the cold. In the past, it was used to make goods such as soap and oil for household lighting.

Breaching is another term for leaping clear above the water.

Camouflage is used by animals to hide themselves in their surroundings. For example, the winter coat of an Arctic fox is white and makes it invisible against the snow. Camouflage helps to protect an animal from predators and also helps it to capture prey.

Carnivores are meat-eating animals.

Floes are pieces of frozen sea water. Some are a few metres long – others are 10km in length!

Germination is the moment when plant seeds begin to sprout. They are roused from their dormant state by suitable conditions for growth.

Glacier is a river of ice that moves very slowly, pushed by new ice that forms on higher ground.

Greenhouse gases such as carbon dioxide, collect in the Earth's atmosphere. They trap heat rays from the Sun and prevent them from bouncing back into outer space. Because of this, the Earth's climate may be growing warmer.

Growlers are chunks of ice that are smaller than bergy bits. Growlers get their name because of the growling noise they make as they float in the sea.

Herbivores are plant-eating animals.

Iceberg is a large lump of ice that floats in the sea. Many icebergs are chunks of ice that have broken off glaciers. Usually, only 10 per cent of an iceberg shows above the surface of the water.

Icecap is a name for the huge shield of ice that covers both the Arctic Ocean and Antarctica.

Ice flowers form when salt is pushed out as the sea freezes. The salt forms arrangements of beautiful crystals.

Ice sheet is another name for a continental glacier.

Incubation is the time between the laying of a bird's egg and its hatching. The parents normally sit on the egg to keep it warm as it develops.

Meltwater is the water that appears when ice and snow melt in summer. In some areas, meltwater can cause flooding.

Meteorologists study the Earth's atmosphere.

Nomads are tribespeople, such as the Lapps of northern Scandinavia, who do not have a settled home. Instead, they follow their herds of animals in search of fresh pasture.

Ozone layer prevents the Sun's harmful ultraviolet rays from entering the Earth's atmosphere. A hole in this layer is forming over each pole.

Pack ice is made up of pieces of frozen sea water called floes.

Pelt is another name for an animal's fur.

Permafrost is an underground layer of soil that remains frozen all year, even during the polar summer.

Plates are huge sections of the Earth's crust that contain the continents. These plates move slowly, over hundreds of thousands of years. As the plates meet and their edges grind against each other, volcanoes erupt and earthquakes occur.

Subarctic describes the area south of the Arctic. Winter in the subarctic is very cold but summer here is warmer than in the Arctic.

Tabular icebergs have large, flat surfaces like that of a table.

Toothed whales have peg-like teeth. They eat animals such as seals, squid and fish.

Tree line is the furthest point to the north, beyond which the climate is too inhospitable for trees to grow.

Tundra is the belt of land between the Arctic ice sheet and the tree line. The word 'tundra' comes from a Finnish word meaning 'barren land'. Rough scrub is the only vegetation here and the land is characterised by lakes, bogs and streams.

Work book

Photocopy this sheet and use it to make your own notes.

Work book

Photocopy this sheet and use it to make your own notes.

Loading your INTERFACT disk

INTERFACT is easy to load. But, before you begin, quickly run through the checklist on the opposite page to ensure that your computer is ready to run the program.

Your INTERFACT CD-ROM will run on both PCs with Windows and on Apple Macs. To make sure that your computer meets the system requirements, check the list below.

SYSTEM REQUIREMENTS

PC
- 486DX2/66 Mhz Processor
- Windows 3.1, 3.11, 95, 98 (or later)
- 8 Mb RAM (16 Mb recommended for Windows 95 and 24 Mb recommended for Windows 98)
- VGA colour monitor
- SoundBlaster-compatible soundcard

APPLE MACINTOSH
- 68020 processor
- System 7.0 (or later)
- 16 Mb of RAM

LOADING INSTRUCTIONS

You can run INTERFACT from the disk – you don't need to install it on your hard drive.

PC WITH WINDOWS 95 OR 98

The program should start automatically when you put the disk in the CD drive. If it does not, follow these instructions.

① Put the disk in the CD drive
② Open MY COMPUTER
③ Double-click on the CD drive icon
④ Double-click on the icon called POLAR

PC WITH WINDOWS 3.1 OR 3.11

① Put the disk in the CD drive
② Select RUN from the FILE menu in the PROGRAM MANAGER
③ Type D:\POLAR (Where D is the letter of your CD drive)
④ Press the RETURN key

APPLE MACINTOSH

① Put the disk in the CD drive
② Double click on the INTERFACT icon
③ Double click on the icon called POLAR

CHECKLIST

● Firstly, make sure that your computer and monitor meet the system requirements as set out on page 40.

● Ensure that your computer, monitor and CD-ROM drive are all switched on and working normally.

● It is important that you do not have any other applications, such as wordprocessors, running. Before starting INTERFACT quit all other applications.

● Make sure that any screen savers have been switched off.

● If you are running INTERFACT on a PC with Windows 3.1 or 3.11, make sure that you type in the correct instructions when loading the disk, using a colon (:) not a semi-colon (;) and a back slash (\) not a forward slash (/). Also, do not use any other punctuation or put any spaces between letters.

How to use INTERFACT

INTERFACT is easy to use.
First find out how to load the program
(see page 40) then read these simple
instructions and dive in!

You will find that there are lots of different features to explore. Use the controls on the right-hand side of the screen to select the one you want to play. You will see that the main area of the screen changes as you click on to different features.

For example, this is what your screen will look like when you play Explore The Polar Lands – an interactive polar landscape, waiting to be visited. Once you've selected a feature, click on the main screen to start playing.

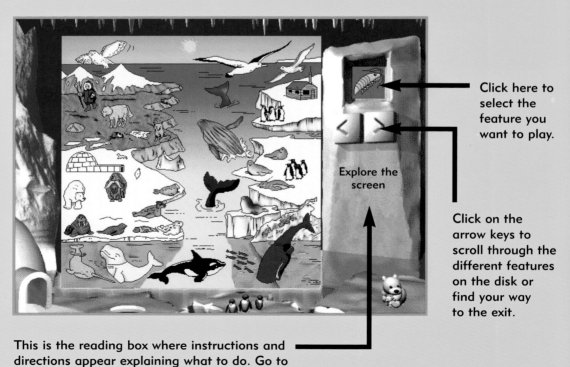

Click here to select the feature you want to play.

Explore the screen

Click on the arrow keys to scroll through the different features on the disk or find your way to the exit.

This is the reading box where instructions and directions appear explaining what to do. Go to page 4 to find out what's on the disk.

DISK LINKS

When you read the book, you'll come across Disk Links. These show you where to find activities on the disk that relate to the page you are reading. Use the arrow keys to find the icon on screen that matches the one in the Disk Link.

DISK LINK
Spot the differences between the Antarctic and the Arctic. They're POLES APART!

BOOKMARKS

As you play the features on the disk, you'll bump into Bookmarks. These show you where to look in the book for more information about the topic on screen. Just turn to the page of the book shown in the Bookmark.

23

WORK BOOK

On pages 36–39 you'll find note pages to photocopy and use again and again. Use them to write down your own discoveries as you go through the book and the disk.

HOT DISK TIPS

- After you have chosen the feature you want to play, remember to move the cursor from the icon to the main screen before clicking on the mouse again.

- If you don't know how to use one of the on-screen controls, simply touch it with your cursor. An explanation will pop up in the reading box!

- Keep a close eye on the cursor. When it changes from an arrow → to a hand ☞ click your mouse and something will happen.

- Any words that appear on screen in blue and are underlined are 'hot'. This means you can touch them with the cursor for more information.

- Explore the screen! There are secret hot spots and hidden surprises to find.

Troubleshooting

If you have a problem with the INTERFACT disk, you should find the solution here. You can also call the helpline on 01933 443 862. The lines are open from 9am to 5pm, Monday to Friday, and calls are charged at normal rates. But remember to get permission from the person who pays the bill before you use the phone.

QUICK FIXES Run through these general checkpoints before consulting COMMON PROBLEMS (see opposite page).

QUICK FIXES

PC WITH WINDOWS 3.1 OR 3.11

1 Check that you have the minimum specification (see PC specifications on page 40).

2 Make sure you have typed in the correct instructions: a colon (:) not a semi-colon (;) and a back slash (\) not a forward slash (/). Also, do not use punctuation or put any spaces between letters.

3 It is important that you do not have any other programs running. Before you start **INTERFACT**, hold down the Control key and press Escape. If you find that other programs are open, click on them with the mouse, then click the End Task key.

QUICK FIXES

PC WITH WINDOWS 95 or 98

1 Make sure you have typed in the correct instructions: a colon (:) not a semi-colon (;) and a back slash(\) not a forward slash (/). Also, do not put any spaces between letters or punctuation.

2 It is important that you do not have any other programs running. Before you start **INTERFACT**, look at the task bar. If you find that other programs are open, click on them with the right mouse button and select Close from the pop-up menu.

APPLE MAC

1 Make sure that you have the minimum specification (see specifications on page 40 for Apple Macintosh).

2 It is important that you do not have any other programs running. Before you start **INTERFACT**, click on the application menu in the top right-hand corner. Select each of the open applications and select Quit from the File menu.

COMMON PROBLEMS

Symptom: Cannot load disk.
Problem: There is not enough space available on your hard disk.
Solution: Make more space available by deleting old applications and programs that you are not using.

Symptom: Disk will not run.
Problem: There is not enough memory available.
Solution: *Either* quit other applications and programs (see Quick Fixes) *or* increase your machine's RAM by adjusting the Virtual Memory.

Symptom: Graphics do not load or are of poor quality.
Problem: *Either* there is not enough memory available *or* you have the wrong display setting.
Solution: *Either* quit other applications and programs (see Quick Fixes) *or* make sure that your monitor control is set to 256 colours (MAC) or VGA (PC).

Symptom: There is no sound (PCs only).
Problem: Your soundcard is not SoundBlaster compatible.
Solution: Configure sound settings to make them SoundBlaster compatible (see your soundcard manual for more information).

Symptom: Your machine freezes.
Problem: There is not enough memory available.
Solution: *Either* quit other applications and programs (see Quick Fixes) *or* increase your machine's RAM by adjusting the Virtual Memory.

Symptom: Text does not fit neatly into boxes and 'hot' words do not bring up extra information.
Problem: Standard fonts on your computer have been moved or deleted.
Solution: Re-install standard fonts. The PC version requires Arial; the Mac version requires Helvetica. See your computer manual for further information.

Index

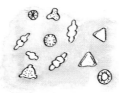